THE
MAGNIFICENT
BOOK OF
BABY
ANIMALS

THE
MAGNIFICENT
BOOK OF
BABY
ANIMALS

Illustrated by
Simon Treadwell

Written by
Barbara Taylor

weldon**owen**

Written by Barbara Taylor
Illustrated by Simon Treadwell

weldon**owen**

Published by Weldon Owen Children's Books
An imprint of Weldon Owen International, L.P.
A subsidiary of Insight International, L.P.
PO Box 3088
San Rafael, CA 94912
www.insighteditions.com

Weldon Owen Children's Books:
Additional illustrations by Fede Combi
Designer: Emma Randall
Editor: Pauline Savage

Insight Editions:
CEO: Raoul Goff
Senior Production Manager: Greg Steffen

ISBN: 979-8-88674-055-4

Manufactured in China.
First printing, July 2024. RRD0724
10 9 8 7 6 5 4 3 2 1

Introduction

From giant giraffe calves to tiny sugar glider joeys, baby animals come in all shapes and sizes. They live in freezing snow, baking deserts, steamy rain forests, watery wetlands, and vast grasslands and even in the busy urban habitats of our world. Some baby animals, such as elephants, stay with their parents for many years, learning the skills they need to survive. Others, such as flatback sea turtles, have to fend for themselves as soon as they are born. It is often the mothers that look after babies, but some fathers, such as African jacanas, take on all the childcare duties themselves. Baby animals that live in groups, such as meerkats, have lots of adults to protect them.

The Magnificent Book of Baby Animals introduces you to a dazzling variety of the biggest, smallest, rarest, most playful, and most unusual animal babies. Discover how a mother American alligator helps her hatchlings to escape from the nest. Marvel at the American flamingo feeding its chicks on pink milk. Find out how a mother hedgehog gives birth to her prickly hoglets. Meet baby Virginia opossums snuggling down in their mother's warm pouch. Admire a wobbly zebra foal standing up only 15 minutes after being born. Take a trip to the South Pole to see how emperor penguin chicks survive in freezing blizzards.

Explore the magnificent world of baby animals and be inspired to help protect these amazing yet vulnerable creatures.

Fact file

Lives: Eastern Africa

Habitat: Grasslands, open woodlands

Height at birth: 6 ft (1.8 m)

Weight at birth: 100–220 lb (45–100 kg)

Lifespan: 25–30 years

Diet: Mother's milk only for 4 months; then leaves, buds, flowers, fruit

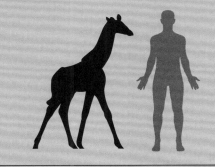

Contents

Emperor penguin chick

Aptenodytes forsteri

🐧 The female emperor penguin lays one egg in May or June, which is winter in Antarctica. The male penguin carefully balances the egg on his feet to keep it off the freezing ice. All through winter storms, he keeps it warm by holding it against a patch of bare skin on his belly.

🐧 After laying her egg, the mother penguin goes out to sea for two months in search of food. By the time the egg hatches, she has usually returned with a belly full of food. She regurgitates, or coughs up, part-digested food to feed to the chick.

🐧 If the chick hatches before the mother returns from her feeding trip, the father feeds the chick himself. He produces a rich, milky liquid from a pouch called a crop in his gullet, or food pipe.

Fact file

Lives: Antarctica

Habitat: Oceans, sea ice, ice shelves

Length of egg: 6 in (15 cm)

Weight at hatching: 5–7 oz (150–200 g)

Lifespan: 15–20 years

Diet: Crop milk, regurgitated fish, squid, and krill; at sea, whole fish, krill, squid

About seven weeks after hatching, emperor penguin chicks have grown a thick, gray fluffy coat of feathers. The little chicks huddle together in a group called a crèche for warmth and protection.

 Emperor penguins are seriously threatened by climate change, which is melting the ice where they nest.

Virginia opossum joey

Didelphis virginiana

- Baby Virginia opossums are called joeys. The mother gives birth to seven or eight joeys after only 12–13 days in the womb.

- Opossum joeys are tiny and not very developed when they are born. They are blind and have no fur. Only their front legs and mouth are well formed.

- Straight after birth, the joeys climb into their mother's fur-lined pouch and cling firmly onto one of her milk teats. They stay here for two months until they are more developed. Mammals that do this are called marsupials.

- Young opossums pretend to be dead if they are threatened or scared. This is known as playing possum. It helps them to survive, because predators prefer to eat live animals.

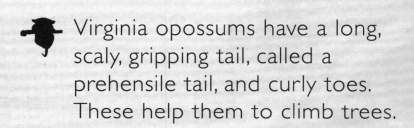

- Virginia opossums have a long, scaly, gripping tail, called a prehensile tail, and curly toes. These help them to climb trees.

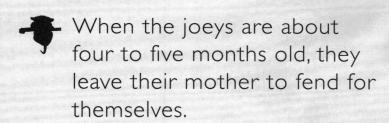

- When the joeys are about four to five months old, they leave their mother to fend for themselves.

Fact file

Lives: Costa Rica, Mexico, USA, Canada

Habitat: Woodlands, wet meadows, deserts, urban

Length at birth: ½ in (1.3 cm)

Weight at birth: $\frac{1}{200}$ oz (0.13 g)

Lifespan: 1.5–3 years

Diet: Mother's milk only for 7–10 weeks; then insects, worms, snails, fruits, nuts, seeds

Roman snail baby

Helix pomatia

- The Roman snail is a type of helix snail. These snails are named after the spiral shape of their shells.

- Roman snails lay 30–60 eggs in a hole in the ground in late spring or early summer. The eggs hatch after three to four weeks. This gives the baby snails plenty of time to grow before the winter. They need to be big enough to survive the cold.

- The tiny babies are almost miniature copies of their parents. The only difference is that their shell is soft and translucent, or partly see-through.

- Snail hatchlings stay in their underground nest at first. They eat the remains of their egg, which helps to make their shell hard. Sometimes, they even eat their weaker siblings.

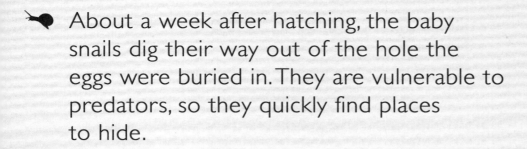 About a week after hatching, the baby snails dig their way out of the hole the eggs were buried in. They are vulnerable to predators, so they quickly find places to hide.

 Roman snails are edible and are part of people's diet in many countries. To protect them, some places limit the numbers that can be harvested.

Fact file

Lives: : Europe, Asia, Africa, North, Central, and South America

Habitat: Woodlands, shrublands, grasslands, sand dunes, scrublands, urban

Length of egg: ¼ in (6 mm)

Weight at hatching: $\frac{7}{1000}$ oz (0.2 g)

Lifespan: 3–10 years

Diet: Leaves, fruits, flowers, tree sap

Cheetah cub

Acinonyx jubatus

Cheetah cubs are born with a fluffy silvery-gray mane along their backs called a mantle. The mantle helps to disguise the cubs' shape in long grass, keeping them safe from predators.

There are 2–6 cheetah cubs in each litter. A mother cheetah looks after her cubs until they are 15–24 months old before she leaves to start a new family. After this, the cubs usually stay together for several more months.

When she goes hunting, the mother cheetah leaves her newborn cubs in a nest hidden in the tall grass. She moves the tiny cubs every few days to avoid attracting the attention of lions, jackals, hyenas, and birds of prey.

Cheetah mothers carry their newborn cubs in their mouth. They hold them by the loose skin at the back of their necks.

Fact file

Lives: Central, eastern, and southern Africa, Iran

Habitat: Grasslands, scrub forests, farmland

Length at birth: 12 in (30 cm)

Weight at birth: 8–15 oz (240–425 g)

Lifespan: 7–12 years

Diet: Mother's milk for 3–6 months; starts eating meat at 5–6 weeks

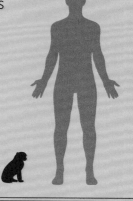

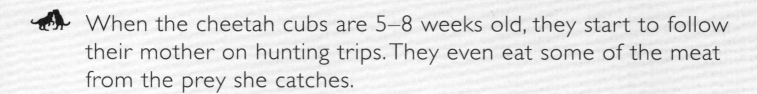 When the cheetah cubs are 5–8 weeks old, they start to follow their mother on hunting trips. They even eat some of the meat from the prey she catches.

Playing with each other helps the cubs to develop their stalking, chasing, pouncing, and wrestling skills. They will need these skills when they start to catch prey on their own.

Himalayan cuckoo chick

Cuculus saturatus

- A female Himalayan cuckoo lays one egg at a time in the nests of other birds. These birds become her chick's foster parents. She does not look after her eggs or chicks herself.

- The Himalayan cuckoo's eggs look similar to foster birds' eggs, but they are bigger. This means they hatch earlier, which gives the cuckoo chick a head start over the foster bird's chicks.

- Sometimes, the cuckoo chick pushes the foster bird's eggs and chicks out of the nest. It then gets all the food and attention for itself.

- The foster birds appear not to notice the cuckoo chick's bigger size and different appearance. They are tricked into feeding and looking after a loud, greedy chick that is not their own.

Fact file

Lives: Himalayas, northern Myanmar, southern and eastern China (breeding); Southeast Asia (migration and winter)

Habitat: Forests, grasslands, plantations, gardens, swamps

Length of egg: ¾–1 in (2–2.5 cm)

Weight at hatching: ³⁄₅₀ oz (1.75 g)

Lifespan: 6–7 years

Diet: Caterpillars and other insects, fruits, berries, plants, birds' eggs

The edges of a cuckoo chick's mouth are orange with black patches. Bright colors often mean an animal is poisonous, so this may help to stop predators from attacking the chick.

The Himalayan cuckoo chick develops its feathers quickly. It is able to fly away from its foster parents' nest when it is only about 17–19 days old.

Flatback sea turtle hatchling

Natator depressus

Flatback sea turtles are named after the shape of their shell, or carapace. This is less domed than the shells of the other six sea turtle species. All types of sea turtle are endangered.

Baby flatback sea turtles grow inside large eggs. The adult female buries her eggs in a nesting pit on a beach before returning to the ocean. Each nest contains about 50 eggs, and it takes eight weeks in the hot sand before the turtles are ready to hatch.

The hatchling turtles have to fend for themselves. First, they dig their way out of their sandy nest. Then they dash across the beach to the sea, doing their best to avoid being caught by night herons, pelicans, sand monitor lizards, feral pigs, and crabs.

Fact file

Lives: Northern Australia, New Guinea

Habitat: Coastal waters, beaches

Length at birth: 2½ in (6 cm)

Weight at birth: 1½ oz (40 g)

Lifespan: About 50 years

Diet: Plankton, sea cucumbers, jellyfish, shrimp, crabs, soft corals, some seagrasses

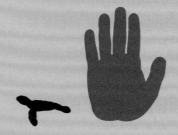

Flatback hatchlings are larger and live closer to the shore than most other hatchling sea turtles. Their size makes them strong swimmers and helps to protect them from shoreline predators such as saltwater crocodiles, sharks, and other fish.

Male hatchlings never return to shore, spending the rest of their lives at sea. Only the females will visit dry land again when they come to lay their own eggs, usually on the same beach they hatched on themselves.

Southern white rhinoceros calf

Ceratotherium simum

Female southern white rhinoceroses, or rhinos for short, give birth to single calf after a pregnancy lasting about 16 months. The calf is born without horns so its mother can give birth more easily.

At birth, the white rhino calf is quite wobbly on its feet. After a few days, it is steadier and can follow its mother around.

The calf's two horns start to grow when it is a couple of months old. They keep growing throughout its long life.

Fact file

Lives: Southern and eastern Africa

Habitat: Grasslands, shrublands, savannas

Length at birth: 21–26 in (55–65 cm)

Weight at birth: 88–143 lb (40–65 kg)

Lifespan: Up to 50 years

Diet: Mother's milk only for 8 weeks; then starts eating grass

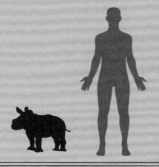

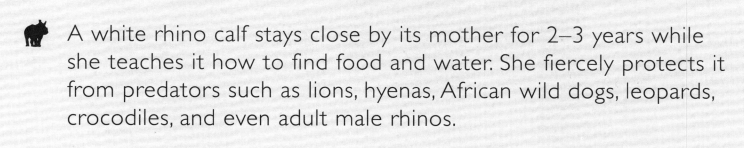 A white rhino calf stays close by its mother for 2–3 years while she teaches it how to find food and water. She fiercely protects it from predators such as lions, hyenas, African wild dogs, leopards, crocodiles, and even adult male rhinos.

Baby rhinos are playful and often practice charging at things around them. This helps them learn how to defend themselves when they grow up.

White rhinos have been brought back from the brink of extinction, but they are still in danger. They are often killed illegally for their horns, which are used in traditional medicines. Expanding protected areas could help them to survive.

Fire salamander larva

Salamandra salamandra

- Fire salamanders are lizardlike creatures with striking yellow-and-black markings. They are amphibians, which means they live both on land and in fresh water.

- Baby fire salamanders grow inside an egg and are called larvae, or a larva when there is just one. The eggs develop for 2–5 months inside the adult female salamander's body. She lays them in water just as the larvae are about to hatch.

- The salamander larvae spend this part of their lives underwater. They go hunting for small water creatures to eat immediately after they have hatched.

Fire salamander larvae look different from their parents—they are more like fish. They have a swimming tail and feathery gills on the outside of their body so that they can breathe underwater.

After 3–6 months, the larvae are ready to live on land. Their bodies go through a big change called metamorphosis. The larvae lose their gills and develop lungs. The shape of their head also changes, and they develop the warning yellow-and-black colors of the adult fire salamander.

Fact file

Lives: Europe

Habitat: Near water in forests and woodlands

Length at hatching: 1–1½ in (2.5–4 cm)

Weight at hatching: ½₅₀–⁷⁄₅₀₀ oz (0.13-0.4 g)

Lifespan: At least 20 years

Diet: Water fleas, worms, insect larvae

Hazel dormouse gray

Muscardinus avellanarius

- The mother hazel dormouse gives birth to 3–7 babies each summer. She makes a ball-shaped nest woven from honeysuckle bark and leaves.

- Newborn hazel dormice have no fur. After about 12 days, they have grown a coat of pale gray fur and are called grays. Their fur turns golden brown as they grow.

- The *hazel* part of this sleepy little rodent's name refers to one of its favorite foods—the hazelnut. The dormouse makes round holes in hazelnut shells with its strong, sharp front teeth to reach the nut inside.

- Young dormice are agile acrobats. They use their long toes and sharp claws to climb plant stems, twigs, and tree trunks. Their paws turn sideways to help them grip.

Fact file

Lives: : Europe, western Asia

Habitat: Woodlands, hedgerows

Length at birth: 1¼ in (3 cm)

Weight at birth: ¼ oz (5 g)

Life span: Up to 5 years

Diet: Mother's milk only for 3 weeks; then insects, flowers, nuts, seeds, berries

Hazel dormice are in danger because their habitat is being destroyed. Conservationists are helping them by putting up nestboxes for them to sleep in. They are also building wildlife bridges so they can cross dangerous open spaces safely.

Eurasian otter pup

Lutra lutra

- Otter pups are born in a sheltered den called a holt. There are two or three pups in each litter. The mother raises them without help from the father.

- The mother Eurasian otter takes her pups out of their den when they are about 10–12 weeks old. They have to learn how to swim, but their fluffy coat makes this difficult. The little pups sometimes have to be dragged into the water by their mother.

- Eurasian otters are endangered. Numbers have increased in places where rivers have become cleaner and the otters are protected.

Otters are playful and curious animals, both as pups and as adults. They chase each other in the water and often enjoy making slides in mud or in snow.

Mother otters teach their pups how to hunt by catching fish themselves and releasing them back into the water for the pups to chase and catch.

Otter pups "talk" to their mother and siblings by making whistling, twittering, spitting, and murmuring sounds.

Fact file

Lives: Europe, Asia, northern Africa

Habitat: Rivers, lakes, swamps, coasts, rice fields, urban

Length at birth: 5 in (13 cm)

Weight at birth: 3½ oz (100 g)

Lifespan: 3–10 years

Diet: Mother's milk for 3 months; starts to eat fish at 7 weeks

Giant panda cub

Ailuropoda melanoleuca

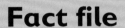 A baby giant panda is blind, toothless, and completely helpless when it is born. The cub is about the size of a mouse—900 times smaller than its mother.

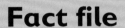 A mother panda cuddles her tiny, fragile newborn close to her body all the time to keep it warm. She feeds the cub on her rich milk and licks it to keep it clean.

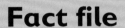 At birth, giant panda cubs are pink, wrinkly, and hairless. It is not until they are about a month old that their black-and-white fur pattern is fully developed. Each cub's markings will be different from any other panda's.

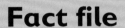 At 10 weeks, a giant panda cub's legs are strong enough for it to crawl. By five months, it can walk, run, and play with its mother.

Fact file

Lives: Southwestern China

Habitat: Mountain bamboo forests

Length at birth: 6–7 in
(15–17 cm)

Weight at birth: 3½–7 oz
(100–200 g)

Lifespan: 15–20 years

Diet: Mother's milk only for 6–8 months; then bamboo, with some insects, eggs, and small animals

Giant pandas are at risk of extinction due to climate change and habitat loss. Scientists are working hard to protect the panda's bamboo forests. They also breed pandas in captivity so they can be released back into the wild.

Older giant panda cubs are good at climbing trees. Their black-and-white colors make it hard for predators to spot them when they are resting or asleep high in the branches.

American flaminglet

Phoenicopterus ruber

🐦 A baby flamingo is called a flaminglet or a chick. Flamingo mothers lay one large egg on top of a cone-shaped mound of mud. The egg hatches after about a month.

🐦 When it first hatches, the flaminglet is only the size of a tennis ball. It grows fast and is as big as the adults by the time it is six months old.

🐦 Flamingos are known for being bright pink, but flaminglets are covered with grayish-white down at first. They slowly turn pink over the next 2–3 years. This is because of the pink shrimp in their diet.

🐦 Flaminglets are born with a straight bill. This helps them to break out of their egg and feed easily from their parents. When the chick is about two weeks old, its bill begins to curve downward.

Both flamingo parents feed their young on a bright pink "milk". They make this in a pouch, or crop, near the top of their food pipe and drip it into the flaminglet's mouth.

Fact file

Lives: Mexico, the Caribbean, northern tip of South America, Galápagos Islands

Habitat: Shallow saltwater lakes and lagoons, mud flats

Length at hatching: 2 in (5 cm)

Weight at hatching: 4–5 oz (115–140 g)

Lifespan: 20–30 years

Diet: Crop milk only for 5–12 days; then brine shrimp, snails, brine flies, worms, algae, seeds

African wild dog pup

Lycaon pictus

- African wild dog pups are born into a pack of 5–20 animals. Only the most important female in the pack has pups. She usually gives birth to around 10 pups per litter, but can have up to 21.

- All the dogs in a pack are related to each other and have close bonds. The other members provide food for the new mother and her babies.

- When the pups are 10–12 weeks old, they leave the underground den they were born in. They follow the adults when they team up to chase and catch animals.

Fact file

Lives: Central, eastern, and southern Africa

Habitat: Grasslands, semideserts, open woodlands, mountains, savannas

Length at birth: 5–6 in (13–15 cm)

Weight at birth: 10 oz (300 g)

Lifespan: 10–12 years

Diet: Mother's milk for 5 weeks; from 3–4 weeks, meat from antelopes, wildebeest, ostriches, hares, birds

After a successful hunt, the adults let the young pups eat first. They stand guard, watching out for predators such as lions.

Female African wild dogs leave their birth pack when they are about three years old. Males remain with the pack and are often left to babysit any pups while the mother joins the pack for a hunt.

African wild dogs are seriously endangered. Conservation groups are working to create wildlife reserves for them and to help farmers live alongside these precious animals.

Tarsier infant

Tarsius spp.

- Tarsiers are primates, which is the same animal group as lemurs and monkeys. They are tiny—adults are only the size of a tennis ball—and are nocturnal, or active at night.

- Female tarsiers give birth to one baby at a time. The infant is about one-third her weight. Even though its actual size is very small, it is the largest mammal baby when compared to the size of the mother.

- Infant tarsiers are born covered in soft, velvety fur. Their enormous eyes are open from the start.

- When they are only a day old, tarsier infants can already jump and climb trees. This helps them to escape predators, such as cats, birds of prey, and snakes.

- All species of tarsier are in danger of extinction, mainly due to habitat destruction. These shy animals are difficult to breed in zoos, so the best way to conserve them is to protect their rain forest homes.

- From birth, tarsiers have sticky pads on the ends of their long, thin fingers and toes. They use these to grip branches and vines.

- Each one of the infant tarsier's huge eyes weighs as much as its brain. It has excellent eyesight, as well as very good hearing. This helps it to survive and hunt in the dark.

Fact file

Lives: Islands in Southeast Asia

Habitat: Rain forests

Length at birth: 1–2 in (2.5–5 cm)

Weight at birth: 1–2 oz (30–60g)

Lifespan: 12–20 years

Diet: Mother's milk only for 4–8 weeks; then insects, frogs, lizards, small birds

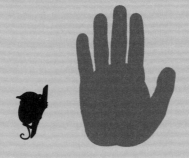

American alligator hatchling

Alligator mississippiensis

- Mother alligators build huge nest mounds using plants, leaf litter, sticks, and mud. They lay 20–60 eggs in the nest. As the plants rot down, the nest heats up, helping the babies inside the egg to develop.

- The temperature inside a nest controls whether the hatchling alligators will be male or female. Lower temperatures produce more females, while higher temperatures result in more males.

- It takes about two months before baby alligators are ready to hatch. They make a high-pitched whimpering sound before punching a hole in the eggshell using a hard, pointed egg tooth on their snout. Their mother hears their calls and uncovers the nest to set the hatchlings free.

Unusually for a reptile, female alligators are caring mothers. They guard the nest and aggressively defend the young alligators until they are 1–3 years old.

Alligator hatchlings can swim from birth. At first, their mother gently carries them in her mouth from the nest to the edge of the water. This helps to protect them from herons, snakes, or even other adult alligators.

Hatchlings are in constant danger from predators. They stay together in a group called a pod for 1–2 years because there is safety in numbers.

Fact file

Lives: Southeastern USA

Habitat: Swamps, marshes, rivers, lakes, canals, reservoirs

Length at birth: 6–10 in (15–25 cm)

Weight at birth: 2–2¼ oz (56–65 g)

Lifespan: Up to 50 years

Diet: Insects, worms, small fish, shrimp, snails at first; then bigger fish, frogs, turtles, birds, small mammals

African pygmy hedgehog hoglet

Atelerix albiventris

- On average, female African pygmy hedgehogs give birth to 3–5 babies, called hoglets, each year. The pregnancy lasts 5–6 weeks.

- Newborn hoglets have 100–150 bendy white spines just below their loose skin. This is so they do not injure their mother during the birth process. After a few hours, these sharp spines break through the skin and start to stand up.

- At birth, the hoglet's eyes are closed. They start to open when it is about two weeks old.

- The smallish white spines the hoglet was born with start to be replaced after about two weeks by longer, stronger spines.

- The hoglet's adult spines—brown, with cream or white tips—appear when it is 2–3 months old.

- Hoglets sometimes spread frothy spit, or saliva, all over their spines. Scientists think this unusual behavior helps them to get attention from their mother or to defend themselves from predators.

- When they are only 6–7 weeks old, the hoglets leave their mother to start an independent life on their own.

Fact file

Lives: Central and East Africa

Habitat: Grasslands, open woodlands, fields, mountains, farmland

Length at birth: ¾–1 in (2–2.5 cm)

Weight at birth: ¼–½ oz (8–13 g)

Lifespan: Up to 4 years

Diet: Mother's milk only for 3 weeks; then insects, spiders, worms, snails, slugs, lizards, mice, fungi, roots, fruits, scorpions, snakes

Chimpanzee infant

Pan troglodytes

When it is first born, an infant chimpanzee is helpless. It has a strong grip and clings tightly to its mother's tummy fur. She carries the infant everywhere with her and they develop a close bond.

Infant chimps are completely dependent on their mothers for the first 5–8 years of their lives. During this time, they learn all the skills they need to survive.

Chimpanzees live together in groups of 15–120 animals. Young chimps spend a lot of time playing with the other infants. This is how they learn how to behave in chimpanzee society.

Male chimpanzees do not look after the infants, but they will play with them and protect them from danger.

At five or six months, infant chimps are strong enough to ride piggyback on their mother. They do this until they are at least two years old, when they start to explore by themselves.

The chimpanzee is in great danger of extinction because of habitat loss, climate change, and illegal hunting. More must be done to protect our closest living relative.

Fact file

Lives: Central and West Africa

Habitat: Rain forests, woodlands, swamps, wooded grasslands, farmland

Length at birth: 12 in (30 cm)

Weight at birth: 2–4 lb (1–2 kg)

Lifespan: 15–33 years

Diet: Mother's milk only for 3–5 months; then fruit, nuts, seeds, eggs, honey, small amounts of insects and meat

Arctic fox kit

Vulpes lagopus

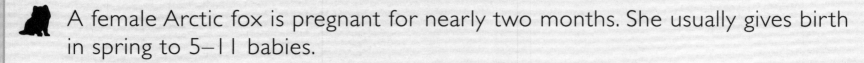

A female Arctic fox is pregnant for nearly two months. She usually gives birth in spring to 5–11 babies.

Baby Arctic foxes are called kits. They are born in a maze of underground tunnels called a den. They cannot see or hear and have no teeth.

The female Arctic fox feeds the kits on her milk at first and keeps them warm. The male brings her food at this time. The kits emerge from the den when they are 2–4 weeks old and start learning to hunt with their father.

Arctic foxes are well camouflaged all year round. Most have a white coat in winter when there is snow on the ground. In summer, when the snow has melted, their coat turns to brown or gray so that they blend in with their rocky surroundings.

Adults make a yelping sound to warn their kits when predators such as eagles and bears are nearby. The Arctic foxes will run to the safety of their den.

When the kits are 4–6 weeks old, they start to eat meat. Both parents are kept busy hunting to provide the hungry kits with enough to eat.

The young foxes leave the family when they are 9–10 months old.

Fact file

Lives: North of the Arctic Circle

Habitat: Arctic tundra, coastal sea ice

Length at birth: 6 in (15 cm)

Weight at birth: 2 oz (57 g)

Lifespan: 3–6 years

Diet: Mother's milk only for 4 weeks; then lemmings, ground squirrels, fish, birds, eggs, plants, berries

Sugar glider joey

Petaurus breviceps

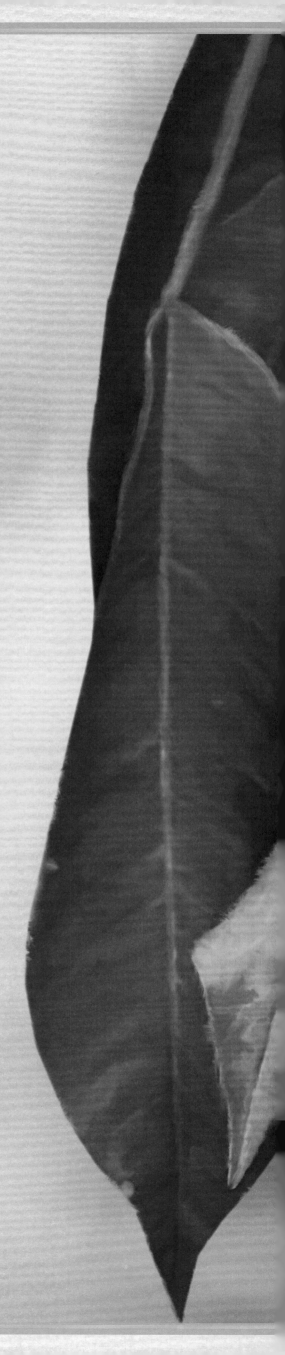

Sugar gliders are very small mammals that live in trees. They have flaps of skin connecting their forelegs to their hind legs. When they spread their limbs, the flaps act like a parachute, allowing them to glide from tree to tree.

Female sugar gliders are pregnant for only 15–17 days. They give birth to one or two babies, called joeys. These are as tiny as grains of rice.

Sugar gliders are marsupials. This means that newborns continue to develop in a pouch on their mother's body.

At birth, sugar glider joeys have no fur and their eyes are closed. The mother gives off a scent so that the joeys can find their way to the pouch on her belly by smell.

Young sugar gliders are cared for in family groups. These are called colonies.

Sugar glider fathers help to look after their offspring. This is unusual for mammals.

Fact file

Lives: Australia, Tasmania, New Guinea, Indonesia

Habitat: Rain forests, woodlands

Length at birth: ⅕ in (5 mm)

Weight at birth: 7/100 oz (0.2 g)

Lifespan: 5–9 years

Diet: Mother's milk only for 9–10 weeks; then tree sap, tree gum, nectar, pollen, seeds, fungi, fruits, insects

African savanna elephant calf

Loxodonta africana

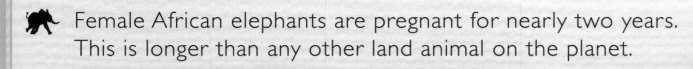 Female African elephants are pregnant for nearly two years. This is longer than any other land animal on the planet.

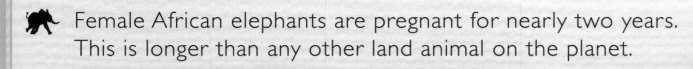 A newborn African savanna elephant calf is more than 30 times heavier than an average human baby. It will continue to grow throughout its long lifetime.

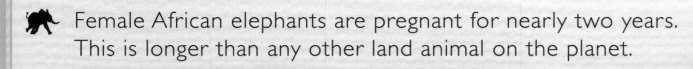 Within a few minutes of birth, the calf has to stand up so that it can reach its mother's milk teat. A baby elephant drinks up to 3 gallons (14 l) of milk each day. Some continue to drink milk for up to 10 years.

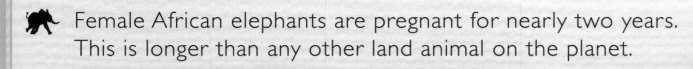 African elephants are endangered. Community projects are helping people realize how precious they are.

Fact file

Lives: Southern and eastern Africa

Habitat: Savannas, grasslands, marshes, scrublands, deserts

Length at birth: 3 ft (1 m)

Weight at birth: 200–250 lb (90–110 kg)

Lifespan: Up to 70 years

Diet: Mother's milk for up to 2 years or more; at about 4 months, grasses, leaves, fruits, bark

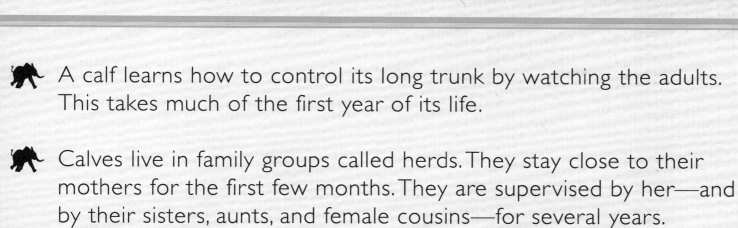 A calf learns how to control its long trunk by watching the adults. This takes much of the first year of its life.

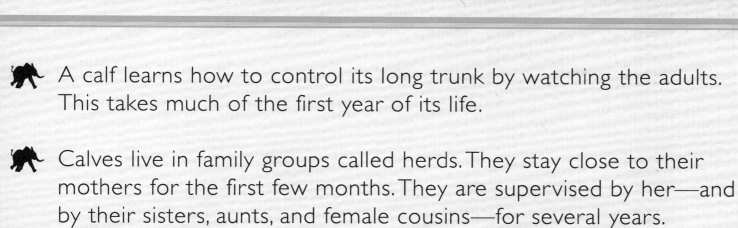 Calves live in family groups called herds. They stay close to their mothers for the first few months. They are supervised by her—and by their sisters, aunts, and female cousins—for several years.

Barn owlet

Tyto alba

- Female barn owls lay about 4–7 eggs once or twice a year. The eggs take about 30 days to hatch.

- Barn owl eggs hatch about two or three days apart so the babies in the nest will be different sizes.

- Baby owls are called owlets. The parents feed the biggest owlet first. This one grows strong and is more likely to survive.

- When barn owlets first hatch, they are nearly naked. Their mother keeps them warm with her body heat for the first two or three weeks. By then, the owlets have grown a coat of warm, fluffy white feathers.

- Father barn owls spend a lot of time hunting for mice, voles, and shrews for the hungry owlets. The mother tears up the food into small pieces to feed it to them.

Fact file

Lives: North and South America, Europe, Africa, India, Southeast Asia, Australia

Habitat: Grasslands, farmland, woodlands, moorlands, shrublands, wetlands, urban

Length of egg: 1½ in (4 cm)

Weight at hatching: 1½ oz (40 g)

Lifespan: 1–5 years

Diet: Small strips of meat at first; at 3 weeks, whole animals, such as voles, shrews, mice

- Barn owlets make a snoring noise to ask for food. They twitter to get their mother's attention or when they are quarreling with other owlets in the nest.

- Barn owlets grow up fast. They leave their parents to start a life of their own by the age of 13–14 weeks.

Masai giraffe calf

Giraffa camelopardalis tippelskirchi

Giraffes are the world's tallest animals, due to their very long legs and neck. Female giraffes have to give birth standing up. If they were lying down, they would squash the calf's neck as it was being born.

As it comes out from its mother's body, the giraffe calf falls nearly 6 feet (2 m) to the ground. This does not seem to hurt the newborn, but the bumpy landing jolts it into breathing for the first time.

A newborn giraffe calf has its eyes open and can stand up in less than one hour. It can feed, walk, and run within 10 hours of being born. This is important, as it needs to be able to escape from speedy predators such as lions, hyenas, and wild dogs.

When giraffes are born, their tiny horns, called ossicones, lie flat against their head to avoid injuring the mother during birth. The ossicones spring up after a few hours.

Satellite tracking has helped scientists to understand giraffe behavior and plan their conservation. Measures include moving giraffes to protected areas so that they do not damage farmers' crops.

Young giraffes are sometimes looked after together by one of the mothers in a crèche, or calving pool. This gives the others a chance to find food and water.

Fact file

Lives: Eastern Africa

Habitat: Grasslands, open woodlands

Height at birth: 6 ft (1.8 m)

Weight at birth: 100–220 lb (45–100 kg)

Lifespan: 25–30 years

Diet: Mother's milk only for 4 months; then leaves, buds, flowers, fruit

Tokay gecko hatchling

Gekko gecko

 The female tokay gecko sticks her eggs to the side of a tree, or underneath a leaf. The eggs take 2–6 months to hatch.

 Both male and female tokay geckos usually guard and protect their eggs and offspring fiercely. They do this until their babies are old enough to live independently at 10–12 months old.

 When a tokay gecko hatches, it sheds a covering of old skin, which peels off its body to reveal a brand-new skin underneath. It usually eats its old skin.

 Tokay geckos are fully developed when they hatch. They have special gripping pads on their toes so that they can climb any surface, as well as a good sense of smell for hunting.

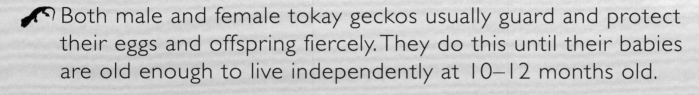

Although they are small, hatchling geckos are often more aggressive than the adults. Their sharp little teeth give a painful bite.

A gecko's top defense against predators is a tail that comes off when in the grip of another animal. This allows the gecko to escape. The gecko will grow a new tail to replace its lost one.

The tokay gecko is protected by laws to prevent it being collected for the pet trade. It is still threatened by habitat loss.

Fact file

Lives: Southeast, South, and East Asia, southern USA

Habitat: Rain forests, deserts, urban

Length at hatching: 2–3 in (5–8 cm)

Weight at hatching: 1/12 oz (2.4 g)

Lifespan: 7–10 years

Diet: Small insects, spiders, worms at first; then larger insects, small rats, mice, baby birds

Raccoon kit

Procyon lotor

🦝 Newborn raccoons, called kits, cannot stand or support their full weight. By the time they are five weeks old, most kits can walk, run, and climb.

🦝 At birth, raccoons have only a very light covering of gray fur and faint black fur over their eyes that looks like a bandit's mask. As they grow, their face mask becomes blacker. Scientists think it reduces glare from their pale fur so that they can see better in the dark.

🦝 There are 2–5 kits per litter. They are looked after by their mother and follow behind her in a line when they move about. They stay with her for up to a year.

🦝 Raccoon kits make a variety of sounds to "talk" to their mother and siblings, such as squeaking, growling, or twittering like a bird. Sometimes, the kits sound like crying human babies.

🦝 Raccoon kits are inquisitive and quickly learn important survival skills by watching and copying their mother. When they are about five months old, they start to hunt for food with her at night.

🦝 Raccoon paws have whiskers near the tips, which makes them very sensitive. Kits rely on their sense of touch to locate their mother and eventually to find their way around by themselves.

Fact file

Lives: North, Central, and northern South America, Europe, Japan

Habitat: Forests, woodlands, mountains, marshes, coasts, grasslands, farmland, urban

Length at birth: 4–6 in (10–15 cm)

Weight at birth: 2–5 oz (60–140 g)

Lifespan: 2–5 years

Diet: Mother's milk only for 6–9 weeks; then insects, worms, fish, crayfish, frogs, birds' eggs, fruit, nuts, rubbish

Prairie dog pup

Cynomys spp.

- The prairie dog is named after its doglike barking calls. This stocky little animal is not a dog at all—it is a rodent.

- Hundreds of prairie dogs live together in groups, or colonies, known as towns. These towns are made up of 15–26 families. Each family consists of one or two males and up to four related females and their young.

- Female prairie dogs give birth to 3–8 pups in a nesting burrow deep underground. The helpless pups have no fur at first. Their eyes are closed for about five weeks.

- When the pups are about seven weeks old, they venture aboveground. They spend their time feeding, playing, and exploring.

- Prairie dogs from the same family greet each other by touching noses and mouths, "kissing" each other, and grooming each other's fur.

- The pups are looked after mostly by the females. The males help to defend their family group from strange males and predators.

- Prairie dog pups are fully grown by five months. The males leave to find a new colony when they are about one year old. Females stay in their birth family for the rest of their lives.

Fact file

Lives: USA, Canada, Mexico

Habitat: Grasslands

Length at birth: 2¾ in (7 cm)

Weight at birth: ½ oz (15 g)

Lifespan: 3–5 years

Diet: Mother's milk only for 7 weeks; then grasses, seeds, leaves of flowering plants

African jacana chick

Actophilornis africanus

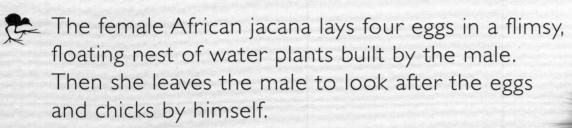 The female African jacana lays four eggs in a flimsy, floating nest of water plants built by the male. Then she leaves the male to look after the eggs and chicks by himself.

The fluffy African jacana chicks leave the nest within four hours of hatching. They can run, swim, dive, and feed themselves straightaway.

The father African jacana removes the broken eggshells from the nest after the chicks have hatched. This stops predators from spotting the pieces of shell and looking for the tiny chicks.

If his chicks are in danger, the father carries them under his wings to a place of safety. He can take up to four chicks at once. Their tiny legs and feet dangle down so that he looks like a bird with many legs.

The jacana's enormous feet and extra-long, thin toes and claws spread out its weight so it can walk easily across water on floating plants, such as water lilies. That is why it is sometimes called a lily trotter.

When they are about six weeks old, African jacana chicks take their first flight. They become independent six weeks after that.

Fact file

Lives: Africa south of Sahara Desert

Habitat: Lakes, rivers, marshes, ponds

Length at hatching: 2–2½ in (5–6 cm)

Weight at hatching: ⅒–⅕ oz (3–5 g)

Lifespan: 5–10 years

Diet: Insects, spiders, shrimps, snails, small crabs, worms

Long-tailed macaque infant

Macaca fascicularis

Long-tailed macaques are born into large groups of 20–100 monkeys. The newborns have black fur. This makes them stand out so the adults know to look after them. When the infants are about three months old, their fur turns gray-brown, like the adults' fur.

Macaque groups contain lots of related females, with a top male in charge. Female infants stay with the same group all their lives, but the males move to another group once they have grown up.

When a long-tailed macaque infant is about six weeks old, it starts to explore on its own. The infant usually stays close to its mother until she has another baby, learning skills like how to use stones to crack open crab shells or hard nut cases.

Long-tailed macaques are endangered because of deforestation and hunting. Some countries have laws to protect them, but more needs to be done to help them survive.

Male infants play with the other young males in the group. They become close friends, and help each other when they grow up and join a new group.

Fact file

Lives: Southeast Asia

Habitat: Forests, mangrove swamps, scrublands, grasslands, mountains, farmland, urban, coasts

Length at birth: 6–7 in (15–18 cm)

Weight at birth: 11 oz (320 g)

Lifespan: 15–30 years

Diet: Mother's milk for at least 1 year; from 2 weeks, some fruit, flowers, leaves, roots, bark, insects, crabs, fish

Red squirrel kit

Sciurus vulgaris

- A female red squirrel has between 3–6 babies per litter. She gives birth in a round nest, or drey, which she builds high up in a tree.

- Baby red squirrels are called kits or kittens. At first, they have no fur or teeth and their eyes and ears are closed.

- Red squirrel kits grow quickly and usually double in size within their first week. Their ears open at the age of about three weeks. Their eyes open later, when they are 4–5 weeks old.

- The kits will not get all their fur until they are three weeks old. Their coat is dark to begin with and does not become its distinctive red color until they are 3–4 months old.

Fact file

Lives: Europe, northern Asia

Habitat: Coniferous and deciduous woodlands

Length at birth: 1–2 in (2.5–5 cm)

Weight at birth: ¼–½ oz (10–18 g)

Lifespan: 3–7 years

Diet: Mother's milk only for 6–8 weeks; then seeds, nuts, fungus, bark, sap, flowers, fruits, eggs, young birds

Mother squirrels look after their kits without help from the father. They fiercely chase away any predators and sometimes move the kits to another nest for safety, carrying them one by one in their mouth.

Kits start to venture from the nest when they are about seven weeks old. The squirrel's long, bushy tail helps it to steer and balance when it leaps from tree to tree and scurries along branches.

Wild boar piglet

Sus scrofa

🐗 Baby wild boars, known as piglets, are born with a thin coat of brown fur with creamy yellow stripes. This pattern helps to camouflage them from predators, such as wolves, badgers, lynx, and adult male wild boars.

🐗 A female wild boar is pregnant for almost four months and gives birth to 4–10 piglets. She can have more than one litter of piglets per year.

🐗 Piglets are born in spring in a mound of grass and leaves. They can walk and run around soon after birth.

🐗 Wild boars live in small groups called sounders. These are made up of 2–5 adult females and one or more litters of piglets.

🐗 Adult females work together to protect the piglets. When a group of wild boars is moving around, the piglets are kept safe in the middle, protected by adults in front and behind.

🐗 Wild boar piglets are born with baby teeth. They develop their adult teeth after a year or two. Their tusks start to show when they are about two years old.

🐗 Wild boars communicate with each other using grunts, squeaks, and chirps. Piglets copy the unique sounds their mother makes, so these noises vary between families.

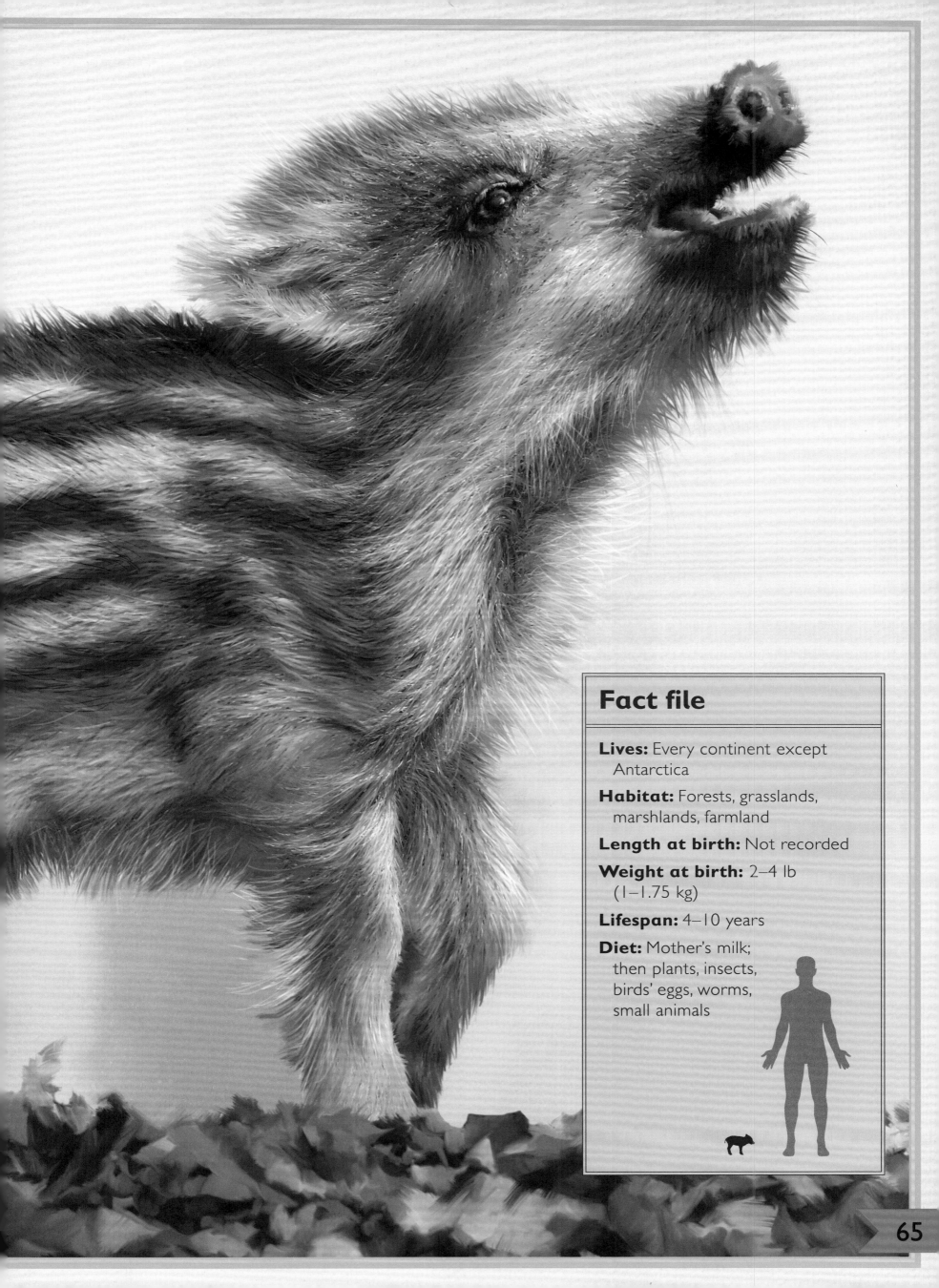

Fact file

Lives: Every continent except Antarctica

Habitat: Forests, grasslands, marshlands, farmland

Length at birth: Not recorded

Weight at birth: 2–4 lb (1–1.75 kg)

Lifespan: 4–10 years

Diet: Mother's milk; then plants, insects, birds' eggs, worms, small animals

Black bear cub

Ursus americanus

- Female black bears give birth to their cubs in January or February while hibernating inside a winter den. They usually have two or three cubs at a time.

- Newborn black bears are covered in fine gray fur. Their adult fur is often black, but can be brown, red, blond, gray or white, despite their name.

- Black bear cubs are born with their blue eyes closed. They open their eyes when they are 4–6 weeks old and start walking soon afterward. The eyes turn brown within a year.

- Mothers take good care of their cubs over the winter, licking them clean, keeping them warm, and feeding them milk. The family emerges from their den in spring, when the weather is warmer.

- When they are anxious, black bear cubs squeal or scream. They make a humming sound when they are comfortable or feeding on milk.

- Black bear cubs stay with their mother for up to 18 months so that she can teach them life skills, such as how to swim.

- Young black bears are very good at climbing trees. They use their curved claws to grip tree bark.

Fact file

Lives: Canada, USA, Mexico

Habitat: Forests, meadows, mountains, swamps

Length at birth: 8 in (20 cm)

Weight at birth: 10–16 oz (280–450 g)

Lifespan: 10–30 years

Diet: Mother's milk for 30 weeks; then grasses, herbs, honey, nuts, fruit, seeds, fish, insects, small animals, deer, dead animals

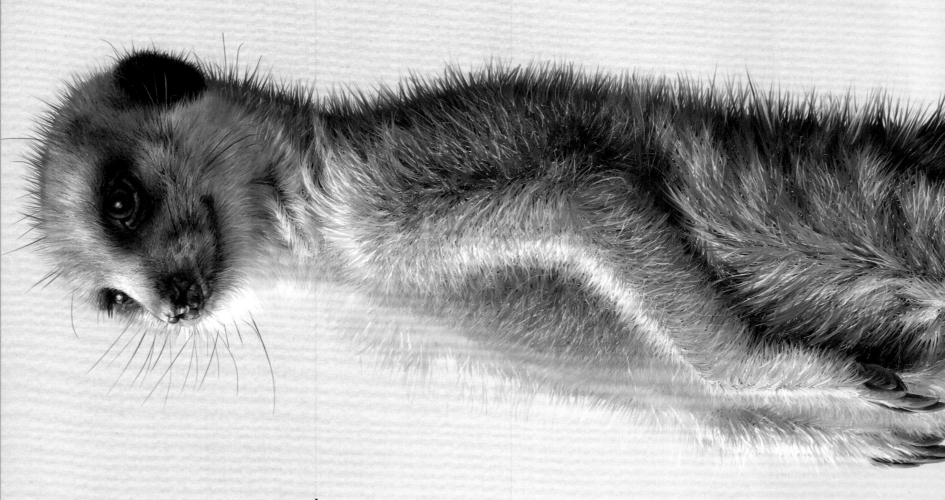

Meerkat pup

Suricata suricatta

Baby meerkats are known as pups. They are usually born in spring and summer, when there is more food available in their dry desert habitat.

About 3–7 meerkat pups are born at a time. They stay inside long underground burrows with their mother until they are about 16 days old.

Meerkat pups have hardly any fur when they are born, and their eyes and ears are closed. By the time the pups are three weeks old, they have grown light brown fur and their eyes and ears have opened.

Meerkats live in family groups called mobs or gangs, which are led by the females. There can be up to 30 animals in the mob, and members help to babysit each other's pups.

Meerkat pups start looking for food with their family group when they are about one month old. Meerkats get all the water they need from their food.

Adult meerkats stand up tall on their back legs to look out for danger. They bark or whistle to warn the pups about predators such as snakes, hawks, eagles, foxes, and jackals. The pups will run to the nearest burrow for safety.

Meerkat pups learn by playing and by copying the adults. The adults also teach the pups special skills, such as how to safely hunt and eat a venomous scorpion.

Fact file

Lives: Southern Africa

Habitat: Deserts, grasslands, shrublands

Length at birth: 2¾ in (7 cm)

Weight at birth: 1 oz (25 g)

Lifespan: 5–15 years

Diet: Mother's milk only for 3–9 weeks; then insects, spiders, eggs, small animals, fruit, roots and tubers

Harp seal whitecoat

Pagophilus groenlandicus

- Female harp seals are pregnant with a single baby for about 11 months. They come out of the water in February to give birth on the sea ice, sometimes taking as little as 15 seconds.

- A baby harp seal is called a whitecoat or pup. It has a yellowy-white coat at first, but after a few days its coat turns pure white. This helps to camouflage the pup from predators.

- Whitecoats grow fast by drinking their mother's rich milk. They put on about 4½ lb (2 kg) every day. After 10–12 days, the mother stops feeding her pup and leaves it to fend for itself.

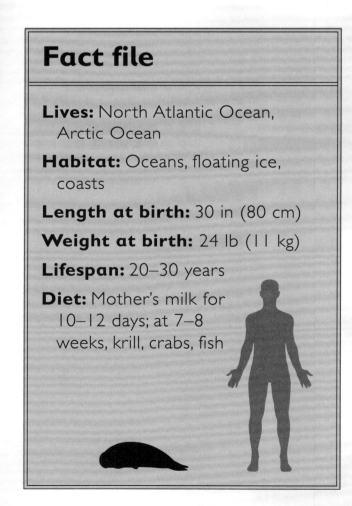

Fact file

Lives: North Atlantic Ocean, Arctic Ocean

Habitat: Oceans, floating ice, coasts

Length at birth: 30 in (80 cm)

Weight at birth: 24 lb (11 kg)

Lifespan: 20–30 years

Diet: Mother's milk for 10–12 days; at 7–8 weeks, krill, crabs, fish

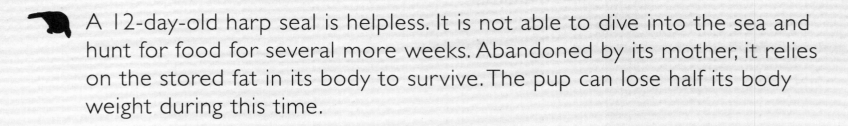 A 12-day-old harp seal is helpless. It is not able to dive into the sea and hunt for food for several more weeks. Abandoned by its mother, it relies on the stored fat in its body to survive. The pup can lose half its body weight during this time.

When they are 3–4 weeks old, harp seal pups shed the white fur they were born with and develop their silvery-gray adult colors. At 13–14 months old, a black harp shape starts to appear on the young seals' backs. This is what gives these seals their name.

Harp seals are noisy animals and make lots of different calls, including whistles, growls, clicks, and trills. Pups call to their mothers by "bawling".

Eurasian lynx kitten

Lynx lynx

Eurasian lynx kittens are born in a sheltered, cozy den lined with feathers, deer hair, and grasses. There are usually two or three kittens in each litter.

When they are about six weeks old, the kittens are strong enough to leave their den. They are active and curious about their surroundings. The kittens are good at climbing, using their sharp claws to cling to trees and rocks.

The mother lynx takes her older kittens with her when she goes hunting at dawn or dusk. By watching her, the kittens learn how to ambush, or surprise, their prey.

Fact file

Lives: Europe, Asia

Habitat: Forests, grasslands, shrublands, mountains

Length at birth: 7–8 in (18–20 cm)

Weight at birth: 8–15 oz (240–425 g)

Lifespan: 10–20 years

Diet: Mother's milk only for 4–6 weeks; then meat from foxes, hares, rabbits, squirrels, birds and deer

Eurasian lynxes are threatened by people cutting down the forests where they live. In some parts of Europe, these secretive wildcats have been reintroduced to protected areas to help them survive.

When the Eurasian lynx kittens are about 10 months old, they are ready to leave their mother. Siblings sometimes travel and hunt together for a few more months.

Indian pangolin pup

Manis crassicaudata

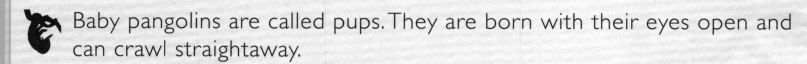 Baby pangolins are called pups. They are born with their eyes open and can crawl straightaway.

Pangolins are covered in sharp-edged scales. A baby pangolin's scales are soft so that it does not hurt its mother while it is being born. The scales start to harden when the pup is about two days old.

Pangolins are hunted illegally for their scales and meat. They are likely to become extinct unless this hunting is stopped. Scientists are trying to find out more about these shy, secretive animals so that they can protect them in the wild.

Pangolin mothers look after their pups inside deep burrows. The pups start to venture outside after about four weeks.

 Until they are about three months old, pangolin pups hitch a ride by hanging onto the scales on their mother's tail.

 If she senses danger, the mother pangolin curls her body around her baby. Her hard scales act like a suit of armor to protect them both.

Fact file

Lives: India, Bangladesh, Pakistan, Nepal, Sri Lanka

Habitat: Forests, farmland, grasslands, deserts

Length at birth: 17 in (42 cm)

Weight at birth: 8 oz (230 g)

Lifespan: (Wild) not recorded; (in captivity) up to 20 years

Diet: Mother's milk for 3–4 months; at 1 month, ants and termites

Cape mountain zebra foal

Equus zebra zebra

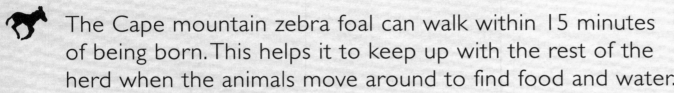

The Cape mountain zebra foal can walk within 15 minutes of being born. This helps it to keep up with the rest of the herd when the animals move around to find food and water.

A newborn's legs are almost as long as its mother's. Their long legs enable them to run away quickly from danger. Foals are especially vulnerable to attacks by fast-moving predators such as lions, hyenas, leopards, and African wild dogs.

Cape mountain zebra foals have soft, fuzzy fur, with brown-and-white stripes at first. The brown parts deepen to black as the foal grows.

Cape mountain zebra foals usually drink their mother's milk for about 10 months. Some suckle for 16–18 months or more.

The smallest of the zebra species, Cape mountain zebras were once on the brink of extinction. They are still vulnerable, so they live in protected national parks.

 Every zebra has its own unique pattern of stripes. Foals must learn their mother's stripe pattern, as well as her smell and call, so that they can follow her for food and protection.

Fact file

Lives: South Africa

Habitat: Mountain grasslands and shrublands

Length at birth: 18–24 in (45–60 cm)

Weight at birth: 55 lb (25 kg)

Lifespan: 18–25 years

Diet: Mother's milk only for 1 week; then taller grasses, leaves, twigs

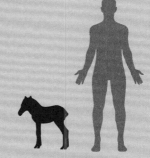

African spurred tortoise hatchling

Centrochelys sulcata

- African spurred tortoise eggs take 4–8 months to hatch. The parents do not look after the eggs or the baby tortoises.

- The baby tortoises are called hatchlings at first. They use a sharp egg tooth on their snout to help them break free of their eggshells.

- When they hatch out, these tiny reptiles are fierce and very active. They push and shove and often try to flip other hatchlings over onto their backs.

- Hatchlings escape the intense daytime heat of the desert by hiding in underground burrows abandoned by other animals. When they are strong enough, they dig their own burrows.

Fact file

Lives: Southern Sahara Desert and northern Africa

Habitat: Grasslands, deserts, shrublands

Length at hatching: 2–3 in (5–8 cm)

Weight at hatching: 1–1½ oz (25–40 g)

Lifespan: 50–100 years

Diet: Grasses, flowers, cacti

These tiny babies grow to be the third-largest species of tortoise in the world. They double in size every three years until they reach adulthood at 10–15 years of age.

African spurred tortoises are endangered. Conservationists are trying to save them by releasing babies born in captivity into protected wildlife reserves.

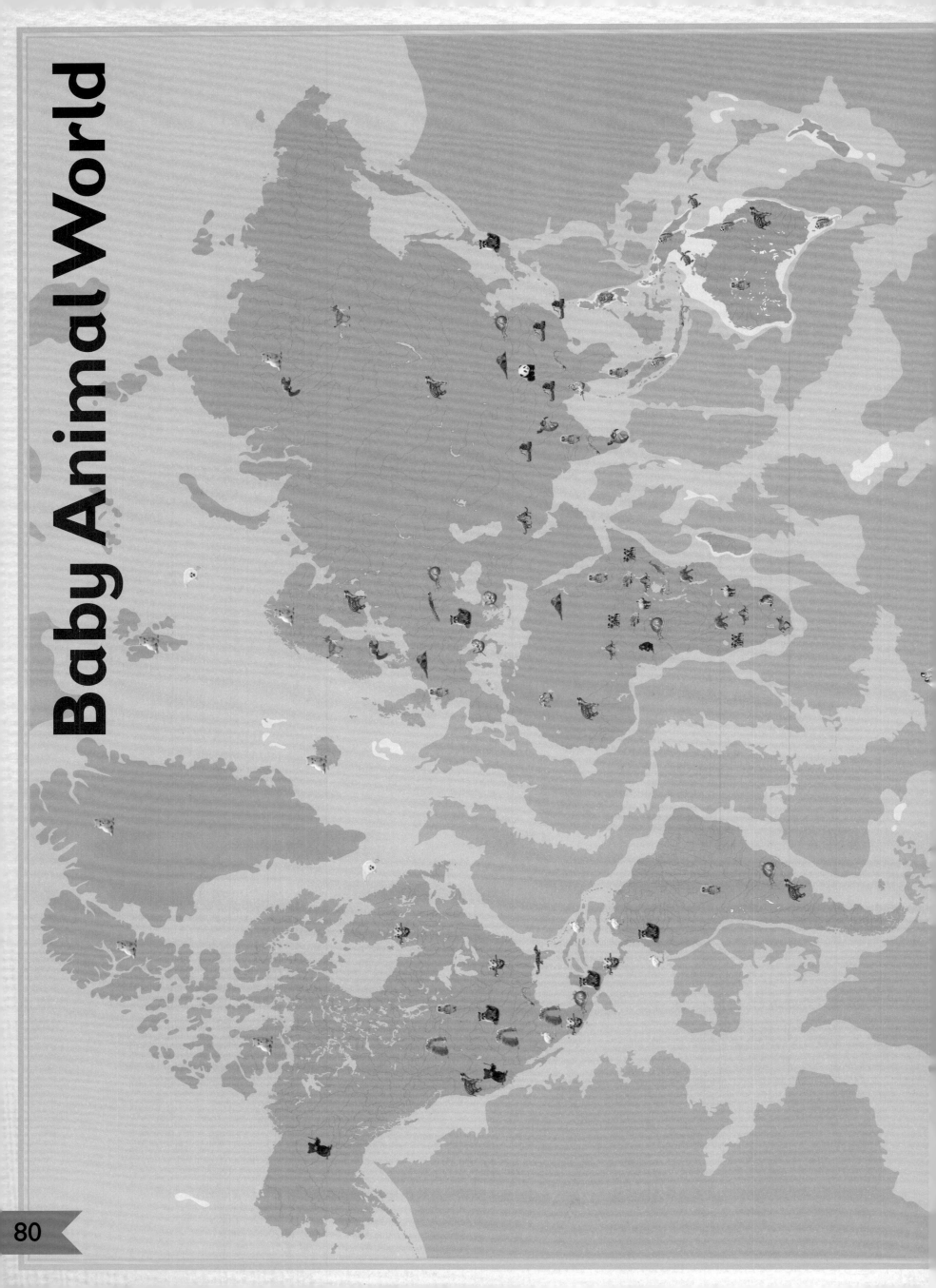